My Love, God Is Everywhere

By Victoria Robb Powers and Cameron Mason Vickrey

Illustrated by Joanna Carillo

Tommy NELSON®

An Imprint of Thomas Nelson

My Love, God Is Everywhere

© 2023 text by Victoria Robb Powers and Cameron Mason Vickrey and illustrations by Joanna Carillo

Tommy Nelson, PO Box 141000, Nashville, TN 37214

Published in Nashville, Tennessee, by Tommy Nelson. Tommy Nelson is an imprint of Thomas Nelson. Thomas Nelson is a registered trademark of HarperCollins Christian Publishing, Inc.

Authors and illustrator are represented by The Christopher Ferebee Agency, www.christopherferebee.com.

Tommy Nelson titles may be purchased in bulk for educational, business, fundraising, or sales promotional use. For information, please e-mail SpecialMarkets@ThomasNelson.com.

ISBN 978-1-4002-4381-5 (eBook)

Library of Congress Cataloging-in-Publication Data

Names: Powers, Victoria Robb, 1987- author. | Vickrey, Cameron Mason, 1983- author. | Carillo, Joanna, illustrator.
Title: My love, God is everywhere / by Victoria Robb Powers and Cameron Mason Vickrey ; art by Joanna Carillo.
Description: Nashville, Tennesse, USA : Thomas Nelson, [2023] | Audience: Ages 4-8 | Summary: "Encounter God's unlimited presence and unconditional love in this joyful picture book inviting kids into all parts of God's creation, from the mountains to the anthills and, most of all, in our hearts amid joy, sadness, calm, and chaos"-- Provided by publisher.
Identifiers: LCCN 2022055891 (print) | LCCN 2022055892 (ebook) | ISBN 9781400243822 (hardcover) | ISBN 9781400243815 (ebook)
Subjects: LCSH: Presence of God--Juvenile literature.
Classification: LCC BT180.P6 P69 2023 (print) | LCC BT180.P6 (ebook) | DDC 231.7--dc23/eng20230222
LC record available at https://lccn.loc.gov/2022055891
LC ebook record available at https://lccn.loc.gov/2022055892

Printed in India

23 24 25 26 27 REP 10 9 8 7 6 5 4 3 2 1

Mfr: REP / Sonipat, India / July 2023 / PO #12167139

To our own loves:

Benjamin, Ruthie, and Hannah
Finley, Zetta, and Sloane
Colette and Miles

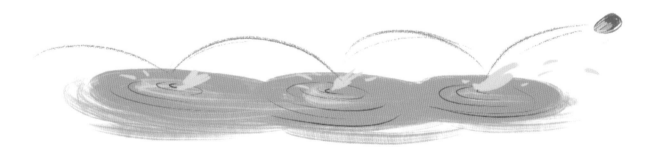

One day I asked my mom,
"Where is God?
Is God here?
Or is God there?"

She said, "My love,

God is everywhere."

Is God way up HIGH

or way down LOW?

My love, God is way up high,
beyond the tallest trees.
God's love is always bigger
than the biggest thing you see.

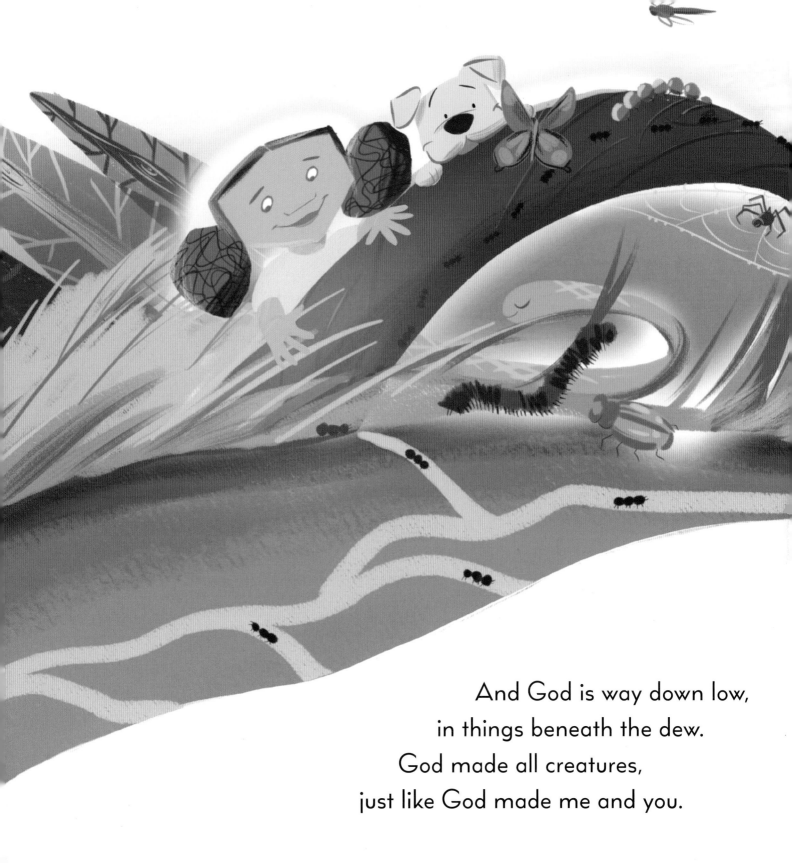

And God is way down low,
in things beneath the dew.
God made all creatures,
just like God made me and you.

Is God here in these FLOWERS

or there with that DOG?

My love, God is in the field of flowers that grow and bring us joy.
Because God is in all nature, connecting with every girl and boy.

And God's warmth is in the dog,
who loves us all day long,

always happy to see us
and forgiving every wrong.

Is God here when it's

LOUD

or there when it's QUIET?

My love, God is here when it's loud,
in the music that we sing.
God is even present
when shouts of chaos ring.

And God is there when it's quiet,
in the stillness that we meet.
When we can't hear a thing,
God is close like our heartbeat.

Is God here when I'm HAPPY

or there when I'm SAD?

My love, God is here
when you're happy,
in your joy
and celebration.
God dances with you
because you are
God's creation.

And God is there when you're sad,
holding you when you're blue,
hurting alongside you
because God gets sad too.

Is God here when I'm SCARED

or there when I'm BRAVE?

My love, God is here when you're scared,
when you're anxious and afraid.
God is here to hold your hand
on days you feel betrayed.

And God is there when you're brave,
when you feel like standing tall.
When you're ready to face dragons,
God is with you through it all.

Is God here when I'm GOOD

or there when I'm BAD?

My love, God is here when you choose goodness
and are living from your heart.
When you follow the path of love,
God is with you from the start.

And God is there when you mess up,
if you make a choice that isn't best.
It doesn't mean you're bad;
it just means you're human—like all the rest.

Is God here
with HER
or there
with HIM?

My love, God is here with her,
    having formed and called her good.
        God dwells in her
            even when she feels misunderstood.

And God is there with him,
having made him wonderfully too.
Because God is in all of us;
it doesn't matter who.

Is God here when I'm ALIVE

or there when I DIE?

My love, God is here with you now,
filling your lungs with every breath.
God is always near, and
nothing can separate you—
     not even death.

Because even when you die,
God's arms are stretched out wide,
ready to wipe away your tears
and greet you on the other side.

"So God is here *and* there?" I asked.

"Yes," she said. "God is always here, and God will always be there."